Anthology 4

William Collins' dream of knowledge for all began with the publication of his first book in 1819. A self-educated mill worker, he not only enriched millions of lives, but also founded a flourishing publishing house. Today, staying true to this spirit, Collins books are packed with inspiration, innovation and practical expertise. They place you at the centre of a world of possibility and give you exactly what you need to explore it.

Collins. Freedom to teach.

Published by Collins
An imprint of HarperCollins*Publishers*
The News Building
1 London Bridge Street
London
SE1 9GF

Browse the complete Collins catalogue at
www.collins.co.uk

British Library Cataloguing-in-Publication Data
A Catalogue record for this publication is available from the British Library

Publishing Manager: Lizzie Catford
Project Managers: Dawn Booth and Sarah Thomas
Copy editor: Dawn Booth
Cover design and artwork: Amparo Barrera and Lynsey Murray at Davidson Publishing Solutions
Internal design: Davidson Publishing Solutions
Artwork: QBS pp.15, 16, 17, 23, 24, 25, 26, 27, 28, 29, 30, 31, 33, 34, 35, 38, 40, 44, 45, 46, 47, 48, 64, 66, 67, 68, 69, 76

Acknowledgements
The publishers wish to thank the following for permission to reproduce content. Every effort has been made to trace copyright holders and to obtain their permission for the use of copyright materials. The publishers will gladly receive any information enabling them to rectify any error or omission at the first opportunity.

Go Ape Leaflet on pp.6–13, www.goape.co.uk, 2015. Reproduced by permission of Go Ape Forest Adventure; Poem on p.15 "I Love Our Orange Tent" by Berlie Doherty from *Big Bulgy Fat Black Slugs*, Thomas Nelson, 1993. Reproduced by permission of David Higham Associates Ltd; Poem on pp.16–17 "The Magnificent Bull" by the Dinka tribe, published in *African Poetry*, translated and edited by Ulli Beier, Cambridge University Press, 1996, p.124, and p.66 "Kob Antelope" translated by Ulli Beier. Reproduced by kind permission of Tunji Beier; Poems on pp.18, 65 "African Elephant" and "Snake in the Grass" by Valerie Bloom from *Jaws and Claws and Things with Wings* by Valerie Bloom, Collins Big Cat, pp.22–23, 28–29, copyright © Valerie Bloom, 2013. Reproduced by permission of Valerie Bloom through Eddison Pearson Limited; An extract on pp.25–28 from *The Diary of a Killer Cat* by Anne Fine, Penguin Books, 2009, pp.1–11. Reproduced by permission of David Higham Associates Ltd; pp.29–32 'The Boy Who Cried Wolf' from *Illustrated Stories from Aesop*, pp.254–262, copyright © 2013 Usborne Publishing Ltd. Reproduced by permission of Usborne Publishing, 83–85 Saffron Hill, London EC1N 8RT, UK. www.usborne.com; pp.34–41 *Snug* by Michael Morpurgo, pp.7–17, copyright © 1995. Reproduced by permission of David Higham Associates Ltd; An extract and two illustrations on pp.42–43 from *Cockadoodle-Doo, Mr Sultana!* by Michael Morpurgo, illustrated by Shoo Rayner, HarperCollins Children's Books, 2010, pp.36–46, copyright © 2010, Michael Morpurgo and Shoo Rayner. Reproduced by permission of David Higham Associates Ltd; Extracts on pp.49–55 from *Stowaway!* reprinted by permission of HarperCollins Publishers Ltd © 2007 Julia Jarman and six illustrations © 2007 Mark Oldroyd; An extract on pp.56–59 from *Sophie's Rules* reprinted by permission of HarperCollins Publishers Ltd © 2011 Keith West; An extract on pp.60–61 from *In the Rue Bel Tesoro* reprinted by permission of HarperCollins Publishers Ltd © 2011 Lin Coghlan and one illustration © 2011 Philip Bannister; An extract on pp.62–63 from *Ade Adepitan: A Paralympian's Story* reprinted by permission of HarperCollins Publishers Ltd © 2013 Ade Adepitan and two illustrations © 2013 Philip Bannister; An extract on p.64 from *The War Orphan* by Rachel Anderson, OUP, 2000, copyright © Rachel Anderson 2000. Reproduced by permission of Oxford University Press; An extract on pp.67–68 from *Angry Arthur* by Hiawyn Oram, 1982. Reproduced with permission of Andersen Press Ltd; An extract on pp.70–73 from *Breath* reprinted by permission of HarperCollins Publishers Ltd © 2013 Claire Llewellyn; Poem on p.76 "What is ... The Sun?" by Wes Magee published in *The Witch's Brew and Other Poems* by Wes Magee, Cambridge University Press, 1989. Reproduced by kind permission of the author Wes Magee; An extract on pp.77–78 from *Black Holes* reprinted by permission of HarperCollins Publishers Ltd © 2013 Anna Claybourne

Photos: t = top; c = centre; b = bottom
p.14 (t): Gregar Rozac/Alamy; p.14 (c) Martin Bennett/Alamy; pp.71–71: Tay Rees/Getty Images; p.72: Flirt/SuperStock; p.73: Klaus Vedfelt/Getty Images; p.77, left: Corbis/Golden Pixells LLC/Pablo Rivera; p.77, right: Getty Images/Fuse; p.78 (t): Steve Evans; p.78 (b): Getty Images/Flickr Open/ Miglena Tsvetkova

Anthology 4

Contents

DON'T JUST TAKE OUR WORD FOR IT...

"The best fun, of course, is to be had on the epic zip wires... It's fantastically liberating to step off the platform, sit back and let the wire do the work as a welcome breeze licks your face. **- THE GUARDIAN**

"Great instructors, very friendly and welcoming! Amazing value for money! Loved it... Want to book again already!

- TONI, BRACKNELL

 Hear it direct from the Gorilla's mouth. See what our customers think of us on TripAdvisor and online at goape.co.uk

HANG OUT WITH US

- Follow the @GoApeTribe
- Share your tree top tales
- Tag your action snaps
- Post your knee knocking videos

OUR DIGITAL JUNGLE INCLUDES...

Search GoApeTribe

BOOK BEFORE Y

Pre-booking is strongly
Book at **goape.co**
(no booking fee charged onlin
or call **0845 838 549**
(a £2.00 booking fee will be

PRICES

 TREE TOP A
Gorillas (16 y
Baboons (10-

 FOREST SE
£40 per ride

 TREE TOP
£18 per per

 ZIP TREKK
£45 per per

OPENING TIMES & PARKING CHA

Visit **goape.co.uk** for the
up-to-date information a
differ for each course.

Book at g
or call 084

6

OUR FA...

This season, live life more adventurously...

Go Ape! TREE TOP ADVENTURE

WHAT IS TREE TOP ADVENTURE?

The multi-award winning and original forest adventure set high up in the canopy. Enjoy two to three hours in the trees, taking on Zip Wires, Tarzan Swings, Rope Ladders and a variety of obstacles and crossings.

JOIN US IF YOU'RE...

- Age 10 or older
- Over 1.4m/4ft 7in tall
- Under 20.5 stone/130kg

WHAT ABOUT SUPERVISION?

Under 16s must be supervised by a participating adult. An adult can supervise two under 16s.

16 and 17 year olds can be unsupervised, but cannot supervise under 16s.

WHAT ABOUT PRICE?

Gorillas (16 years plus) from £31
Baboons (10-15 years) £25

Available at 28 locations UK wide look for the 🌲 on the map overleaf

Go Ape! FOREST SEGWAY

WHAT IS FOREST

It's the epic adventure with Jump on board one of our electric Segways and explo beautiful forests. It's a totall

JOIN US IF YOU'RE...

- Over 7 stone/45kg
- Age 10 or over (you must
- Under 19.5 stone/125kg

WHAT ABOUT SUPERVISI...

Under 16s must be supervi
An adult can supervise up

16 and 17 year olds can rid
supervise under 16s.

WHAT ABOUT PRICE?

£40 per rider

**Available at 1...
look for the 🚶 o...**

MILY TREE

with these fantastic Go Ape adventures.

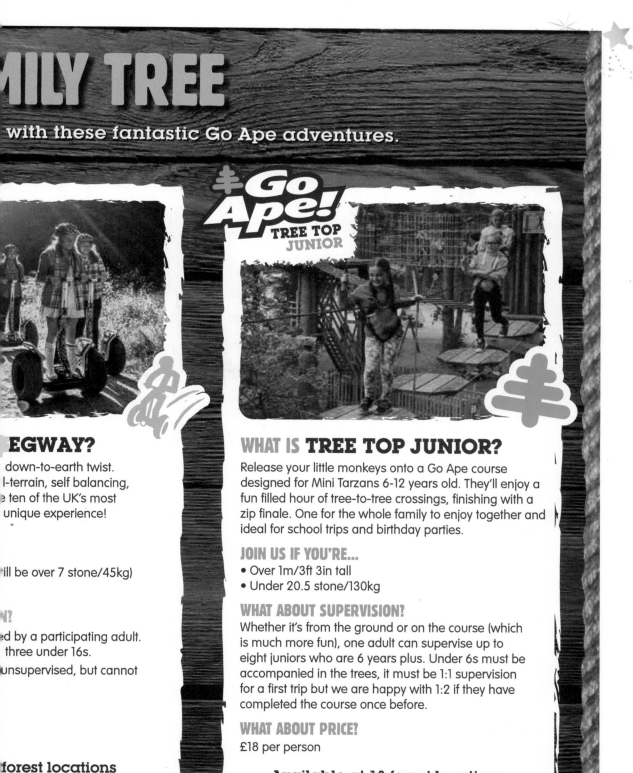

Go Ape! TREE TOP JUNIOR

EGWAY?

down-to-earth twist.
l-terrain, self balancing,
e ten of the UK's most
unique experience!

ill be over 7 stone/45kg)

N?

d by a participating adult.
three under 16s.

unsupervised, but cannot

forest locations
the map overleaf

WHAT IS **TREE TOP JUNIOR?**

Release your little monkeys onto a Go Ape course designed for Mini Tarzans 6-12 years old. They'll enjoy a fun filled hour of tree-to-tree crossings, finishing with a zip finale. One for the whole family to enjoy together and ideal for school trips and birthday parties.

JOIN US IF YOU'RE...
- Over 1m/3ft 3in tall
- Under 20.5 stone/130kg

WHAT ABOUT SUPERVISION?
Whether it's from the ground or on the course (which is much more fun), one adult can supervise up to eight juniors who are 6 years plus. Under 6s must be accompanied in the trees, it must be 1:1 supervision for a first trip but we are happy with 1:2 if they have completed the course once before.

WHAT ABOUT PRICE?
£18 per person

Available at 13 forest locations look for the 🌲 on the map overleaf

BRING THE WHOLE TRIB

CORPORATE EVENTS

A perfect setting for team building and corporate events. Our events team will arrange everything for your Tribe's day.

Get off your lap-tops and into the tree-tops.

Call our events team today 0845 643 6734

CELEBI

Looking
and you
Whether
or Stag/
unforget

Book a

SCHOOL

Our Tree Top
and unforge
pupils. We've
that teacher
Curriculum.
that can be

For more inf

JUNIOR BIRTHDAY PARTIES

Tree Top Junior is ideal for your little Tarzan or Jane's birthday party. Let them loose in the trees, add in Gorilla party bags, a tee for each adventurer and bring your own picnic and cake to have in the forest shelter. It's the best party for any little monkey!

For more information call 0845 643 1689

10

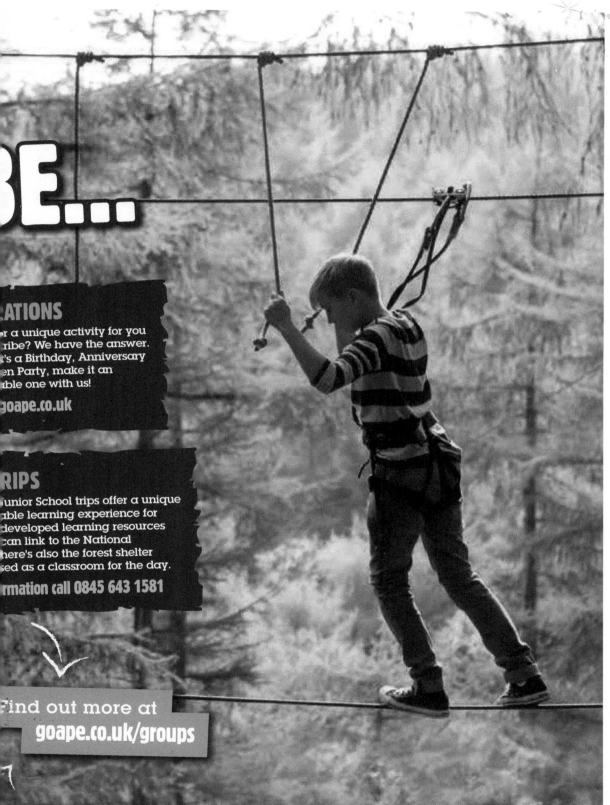

BE...

...ATIONS

...r a unique activity for you
...ribe? We have the answer.
...'s a Birthday, Anniversary
...en Party, make it an
...ble one with us!

...goape.co.uk

...RIPS

...unior School trips offer a unique
...ble learning experience for
...developed learning resources
...can link to the National
...here's also the forest shelter
...sed as a classroom for the day.

...rmation call **0845 643 1581**

**Find out more at
goape.co.uk/groups**

TO THE TREES!
BUT WHICH TREES?

Use the map to find your nearest Go Ape...

Check the icons to find out what's available...

🌲 Tree Top Adventure

🛴 Forest Segway

🌲 Tree Top Junior

🌲 Zip Trekking Adventure

🌲 City Park Adventure

Due to the rural nature of our locations, postcodes are not always accurate when using satnav directions. Please always cross reference with a map.

NEW!

Go Ape Battersea Park, a compact and challenging Tree To

Scotland

01 **CRATHES CASTLE,** NR ABERDEF
Off the A93, 3 miles east of Ban
Follow brown signs for Crathe

02 **ABERFOYLE,** QUEEN ELIZABET
Take the A821 to Aberfoyle an
'The Lodge - Forest Visitor Cer

03 **PEEBLES, GLENTRESS FOREST** N
Take the A72 east from Peeble
After 1.5 miles turn into Glentre

North

04 **NEWCASTLE,** MATFEN HALL H
Take the B6318 Military Road
the A68. Follow signs to Matfe

05 **DALBY FOREST,** NR PICKERINC
Once you reach Pickering or
the brown signs for Dalby the

06 **WHINLATTER FOREST,** NR KESW
Follow the A66 until Braithwai
follow Visitor Centre signs to V

07 **GRIZEDALE FOREST,** NR HAWK!
Approach via Newby Bridge
From Hawkshead follow signs

08 **RIVINGTON,** NR BOLTON
From the M61, follow brown si
Great House Barn, Rivington.

09 **DELAMERE FOREST,** NR CHEST
Exit the B5152 at Delamere Ro
follow the brown signs to Linr

Midlands

10 **BUXTON COUNTRY PARK,** BUXT
From Buxton, follow the brow

11 **SHERWOOD PINES,** NR MANSF
Sherwood Pines is on the B603C
and Ollerton. Follow the browr

12 **CANNOCK FOREST,** NR RUGELEY
Located 2 miles from Rugeley
between Penkridge Bank and

13 **WYRE FOREST,** NR KIDDERMI
3 miles west of Bewdley on th
Forestry Commission signs fro

14 **FOREST OF DEAN,** NR GLOUC
Take the A48 to Blakeney and

Wales

15 **MARGAM COUNTRY PARK,** NR
A short drive from the M4, jun
Follow brown signs to Marga

Book now a

12

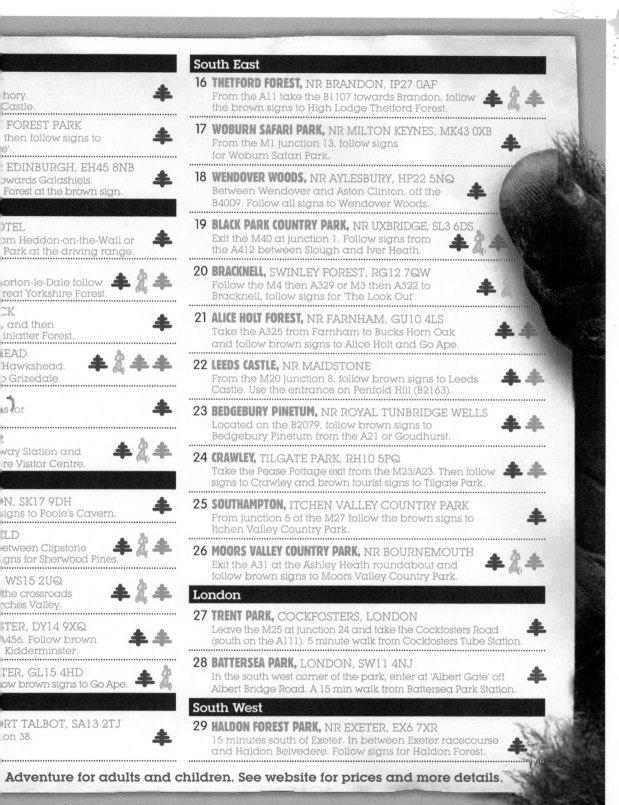

hory.
Castle.

FOREST PARK
then follow signs to
e'.

EDINBURGH, EH45 8NB
owards Galashiels.
Forest at the brown sign.

OTEL
m Heddon-on-the-Wall or
Park at the driving range.

orton-le-Dale follow
reat Yorkshire Forest.

CK
, and then
inlatter Forest.

EAD
Hawkshead.
Grizedale.

s for

way Station and
re Visitor Centre.

N, SK17 9DH
signs to Poole's Cavern.

LD
etween Clipstone
gns for Sherwood Pines.

WS15 2UQ
the crossroads
ches Valley.

TER, DY14 9XQ
456. Follow brown
Kidderminster.

TER, GL15 4HD
ow brown signs to Go Ape.

RT TALBOT, SA13 2TJ
on 38.

South East

16 THETFORD FOREST, NR BRANDON, IP27 0AF
From the A11 take the B1107 towards Brandon, follow
the brown signs to High Lodge Thetford Forest.

17 WOBURN SAFARI PARK, NR MILTON KEYNES, MK43 0XB
From the M1 junction 13, follow signs
for Woburn Safari Park.

18 WENDOVER WOODS, NR AYLESBURY, HP22 5NQ
Between Wendover and Aston Clinton, off the
B4009. Follow all signs to Wendover Woods.

19 BLACK PARK COUNTRY PARK, NR UXBRIDGE, SL3 6DS
Exit the M40 at junction 1. Follow signs from
the A412 between Slough and Iver Heath.

20 BRACKNELL, SWINLEY FOREST, RG12 7QW
Follow the M4 then A329 or M3 then A322 to
Bracknell, follow signs for 'The Look Out'.

21 ALICE HOLT FOREST, NR FARNHAM, GU10 4LS
Take the A325 from Farnham to Bucks Horn Oak
and follow brown signs to Alice Holt and Go Ape.

22 LEEDS CASTLE, NR MAIDSTONE
From the M20 junction 8, follow brown signs to Leeds
Castle. Use the entrance on Penfold Hill (B2163).

23 BEDGEBURY PINETUM, NR ROYAL TUNBRIDGE WELLS
Located on the B2079, follow brown signs to
Bedgebury Pinetum from the A21 or Goudhurst.

24 CRAWLEY, TILGATE PARK, RH10 5PQ
Take the Pease Pottage exit from the M23/A23. Then follow
signs to Crawley and brown tourist signs to Tilgate Park.

25 SOUTHAMPTON, ITCHEN VALLEY COUNTRY PARK
From junction 5 of the M27 follow the brown signs to
Itchen Valley Country Park.

26 MOORS VALLEY COUNTRY PARK, NR BOURNEMOUTH
Exit the A31 at the Ashley Heath roundabout and
follow brown signs to Moors Valley Country Park.

London

27 TRENT PARK, COCKFOSTERS, LONDON
Leave the M25 at junction 24 and take the Cockfosters Road
(south on the A111). 5 minute walk from Cockfosters Tube Station.

28 BATTERSEA PARK, LONDON, SW11 4NJ
In the south west corner of the park, enter at 'Albert Gate' off
Albert Bridge Road. A 15 min walk from Battersea Park Station.

South West

29 HALDON FOREST PARK, NR EXETER, EX6 7XR
15 minutes south of Exeter. In between Exeter racecourse
and Haldon Belvedere. Follow signs for Haldon Forest.

Adventure for adults and children. See website for prices and more details.

goape.co.uk

Home   About   Plan a visit   What's on   Our rides   Restaurants

THRILLS CITY ADVENTURE PARK

Scariest rides ever:

The Brazen Beast   Techno Ride   Raging River's Revenge   Mighty Meteor   Vortex

An awesome day for all the family

- Escape on a once-in-a-lifetime adventure
- Unlimited fun all year round
- New this year – embark on an underwater adventure in the new sea-life aquarium
- Over the Rainbow Club – fab fun for our younger guests
- Live entertainment and characters
- Surprises at every turn
- Splash yourself silly in the water park!
- Stay overnight at our special 4 ★ family-friendly hotel
- Relax in our spa and health club

SPECIAL OFFERS

2-for-1 tickets before 13 July

Family Weekend Autumn Saver

Jump the queues and save 5% – print your tickets at home

OFFERS BY EMAIL

Sign up now to receive the latest information and offers and become a Select Guest

Title:

Surname:

Email:

Sign up

Open 10 a.m. to 6 p.m. every day ★ Close to motorway ★ Free parking

Poetry

I Love Our Orange Tent

I love our orange tent.
We plant it like a flower in the field.
The grass smells sweet inside it.

And at night
When we're lying in it,
I hear the owl crying.

When the wind blows,
my tent flaps
like a flying bird.

And the rain
patters down on it
with tiny footsteps.

I feel warm and safe
inside my tent.

But when the sun is shines,
that's when I love it best!

When I wake up
and the sun is shining,
it pours in like yellow honey.
It glows like gold.

I love our orange tent.

Berlie Doherty

Poetry
The Magnificent Bull

My bull is white like the silver fish in the river
white like the shimmering crane bird on the river bank
white like fresh milk!
His roar is like the thunder to the Turkish cannon on the steep shore.
My bull is dark like the raincloud in the storm.
He is like summer and winter.
Half of him is dark like the storm cloud,
half of him is light like sunshine.
His back shines like the morning star.
His brow is red like the beak of the Hornbill.
His forehead is like a flag, calling the people from a distance,
He resembles the rainbow.

I will water him at the river,
With my spear I shall drive my enemies.
Let them water their herds at the well;
the river belongs to me and my bull.
Drink, my bull, from the river; I am here
to guard you with my spear.

Dinka tribe

Poetry
African Elephant

He's the largest living animal
And the heaviest on the land,
He rips up huge trees by the root
And snaps them like a wand.

The ground shakes where he travels,
Like a mountain rumbling by,
The forest bows before him,
Nothing's above him, except the sky.

Even the king of the jungle
Stands to let him pass,
And people gaze in wonder,
At his power, might and mass.

This animal is an awesome sight,
He's built like a small house,
And yet this mighty elephant
Is frightened of a mouse.

Valerie Bloom

Poetry

The Donkey

I saw a donkey,
One day old,
His head was too big
For his neck to hold;
His legs were shaky
And long and loose,
They rocked and staggered
And weren't much use.

He tried to gambol
And frisk a bit,
But he wasn't quite sure
Of the trick of it.
His queer little coat
Was soft and grey,
And curled at his neck
In a lovely way.

His face was wistful
And left no doubt
That he felt life needed
Some thinking about.
So he blundered round
In venturesome quest,
And then lay flat
On the ground to rest.

He looked so little
And weak and slim,
I prayed the world
Might be good to him.

Anon.

Non-fiction

A Colossal Quake

Recovery efforts continue after a massive earthquake rocks Nepal

By Zachary Humenik with AP reporting

APRIL 27, 2015

A 7.8 magnitude earthquake has caused destruction to buildings and homes in Nepal.

The ground shook on Saturday in the South Asian country of Nepal when the region was hit by a massive earthquake. The quake registered 7.8 on the Richter scale, a 10-point system developed to measure the magnitude, or force, of earthquakes. It was the largest earthquake to strike Nepal since 1934.

While the epicenter of the earthquake was located 50 miles northwest of Nepal's capital city, Kathmandu, it was Kathmandu that suffered significant damage. In much of the countryside, it was worse. The earthquake caused buildings to collapse and triggered an avalanche on Mount Everest, the world's tallest mountain. It was strong enough to be felt all across parts of India, Bangladesh, China's region of Tibet, and Pakistan.

"There are people who are not getting food and shelter," said Udav Prashad Timalsina, a top official in Nepal. "I've had reports of villages where 70 percent of the houses have been destroyed."

So far, more than 4,000 people are known to have lost their lives. About 7,180 people were injured by the quake, police said.

The enormous quake has left many without a home or place to sleep.

Helping Hands

More than a dozen countries and many charity groups are sending aid to Nepal to assist in the recovery. Teams from the United States, China, India, and other countries have traveled to Nepal to help the government with search-and-rescue efforts.

"We have 90 percent of the army out there working on search and rescue," said Jagdish Pokhrel, the Nepalese army spokesman. "We are focusing our efforts on that, on saving lives.

However, many of the affected villages are not easy to reach, as landslides have blocked roads. Another problem is aftershocks. Aftershocks are smaller earthquakes that happen after a larger earthquake. They can often cause additional damage.

Nepal's rescue coordinator Lila Mani Poudyal says aftershocks are delaying rescue crews.

"There have been nearly 100 earthquakes and aftershocks, which is making rescue work difficult," he said. "Even the rescuers are scared and running because of them."

More than a dozen countries and many charities have contributed aid to the people of Nepal. Here, South Korean aid workers prepare to travel to Kathmandu, where fresh drinking water is badly needed.

Aftershocks have also been a concern for Nepali citizens. Many have refused to return to their homes. Afraid that buildings might collapse, many people are sleeping in tents outside.

In a country crippled by this natural disaster, Poudyal is calling for more help from the international community.

"We are appealing for tents, dry goods, blankets, mattresses, and 80 different medicines that the health department is seeking that we desperately need now," he said.

The Accident

SECOND ICE FATALITY IN A WEEK

Tragedy struck again yesterday when an elderly lady fell through the ice. Mrs Wills, of Onslow Gardens, had been walking alone with her sister's dog when it chased a duck onto the frozen river. It is the first time in living memory that the River Thames has frozen from bank to bank.

Onlookers struggled desperately to save Mrs Wills, 79, when she fell through the ice whilst trying to rescue the black Labrador. Rescue services were on the scene within five minutes, but as Chief Officer Chung said, "There was no way anyone could survive more than a minute or two in water with sub-zero temperatures." Last week, the same crew tried unsuccessfully to rescue an eight-year-old boy who had been playing on the ice.

Non-fiction
Holiday Diary

Friday 2 August

Bored, bored, bored! This is our holiday, so you'd think it would be fun. Huh! Raj just sits playing games on his phone all day – he might as well not be on holiday at all, because he doesn't seem to want to go out or play or do anything interesting. Mum and Dad are so exhausted (apparently) that all they really want to do is flop. Still, they've promised to take me to the beach this afternoon. Maybe there'll be someone to play with there.

Later ...

The beach was brilliant! It's really wide, flat and sandy. The sand is excellent for running on, and also for digging and making sandcastles. I had a great time, but you'll never guess what the best thing was. I made friends with this really nice girl, Stacey. She's coming over to our holiday house tomorrow to play.

23

Saturday 3 August

Today was just … amazing. I'm still trying to work out how I feel about it actually. Stacey came over, and we were playing a great game in the garden of the holiday house, when we suddenly noticed a little plane flying overhead. It seemed to be flying a bit low, but we didn't really think about it – until we suddenly saw clouds of smoke billowing out of the back of it! Then, suddenly, it dropped down into the sea. The pilot of the plane must have pressed the 'eject' button because we could see him floating down by parachute. Stacey and I just stared at each other. We were in shock. Then Stacey realised we had to phone for help.

"Meena!" she said. "Grab the phone and dial 999. We need Air-Sea Rescue!" I quickly got on the phone, and told the lady where we were and what we had seen. The lady said they would send a helicopter at once. Sure enough, within minutes we saw a big orange helicopter hovering over the sea where the plane had crashed. A rescue worker was lowered down on a rope, and grabbed the pilot of the plane, who was clinging to the wreckage. Then the pair of them got winched up into the helicopter and flew away.

I hope the pilot is OK. Mum says Stacey and I probably saved his life.

From **The Diary of a Killer Cat** by Anne Fine

1. Monday

Okay, okay. So hang me. I killed the bird. For pity's sake, I'm a **cat**. It's practically my **job** to go creeping round the garden after sweet little eensy-weensy birdy-pies that can hardly fly from one hedge to another. So what am I supposed to do when one of the poor feathery little flutterballs just about throws itself into my mouth? I mean, it practically landed on my paws. It could have **hurt** me.

Okay, **okay**. So I biffed it. Is that any reason for Ellie to cry in my fur so hard I almost **drown**, and squeeze me so hard I almost **choke**?

"Oh, Tuffy!" she says, all sniffles and red eyes and piles of wet tissues. "Oh, Tuffy. How could you **do** that?"

How could I **do** that? I'm a **cat**? How did I know there was going to be such a giant great fuss, with Ellie's mother rushing off to fetch sheets of old newspaper, and Ellie's father filling a bucket with soapy water?

Okay, **okay**. So maybe I shouldn't have dragged it in and left it on the carpet. And maybe the stains won't come out, ever.

So **hang** me.

2. Tuesday

I quite enjoyed the little funeral. I don't think they really wanted me to come, but, after all, it's just as much my garden as theirs. In fact, I spend a whole lot more time in it than they do. I'm the only one in the family who uses it properly.

Not that they're grateful. You ought to hear them.

"That cat is **ruining** my flower beds. There are hardly any of the petunias left."

"I'd barely **planted** the lobelias before it was lying on top of them, squashing them flat."

"I **do** wish it wouldn't dig holes in the anemones."

Moan, moan, moan, moan. I don't know why they bother to keep a cat, since all they ever seem to do is complain.

All except Ellie. She was too busy being soppy about the bird. She put it in a box, and packed it round with cotton wool, and dug a little hole, and then we all stood round it while she said a few words, wishing the bird luck in heaven.

"Go away," Ellie's father hissed at me (I find that man quite rude.) But I just flicked my tail at him. Gave him the blink. Who does he think he is? If I want to watch a little birdy's funeral, I'll watch it. After all, I've known the bird longer than any of them have. I knew it when it was **alive**.

26

3. Wednesday

So spank me! I brought a dead mouse into their precious house. I didn't even kill it. When I came across it, it was already a goner. Nobody's safe around here. This avenue is ankle-deep in rat poison, fast cars charge up and down at all hours, and I'm not the only cat around here. I don't even know what happened to the thing. All I know is, I found it. It was already dead. (Fresh dead, but dead.) And at the time I thought it was a good idea to bring it home. Don't ask me why. I must have been crazy.

How did I know that Ellie was going to grab me and give me one of her little talks?

"Oh, Tuffy! That's the second time this week. I can't bear it. I know you're a cat, and it's natural and everything. But please, for my sake, stop."

She gazed into my eyes.

"Will you stop? Please?"

I gave her the blink. (Well, I tried. But she wasn't having any.)

"I **mean** it, Tuffy," she told me. "I love you, and I understand how you feel. But you've got to stop doing this, okay?"

She had me by the paws. What could I say? So I tried to look all sorry. And then she burst into tears all over again, and we had another funeral.

This place is turning into Fun City. It really is.

27

4. Thursday

Okay, okay! I'll try and explain about the rabbit. For starters, I don't think anyone's given me enough credit for getting it through the cat-flap. That was **not easy**. I can tell you, it took about an hour to get that rabbit through that little hole. That rabbit was downright **fat**. It was more like a pig than a rabbit, if you want my opinion.

Not that any of them cared what I thought. They were going mental.

"It's Thumper!" cried Ellie. "It's next-door's Thumper!"

"Oh, Lordy!" said Ellie's father. "Now we're in trouble. What are we going to do?"

Ellie's mother stared at me.

"How could a cat **do** that?" she asked. "I mean, it's not like a tiny bird, or a mouse, or anything. That rabbit is the same size as Tuffy. They both weigh a **ton**."

Nice. Very nice. This is my **family**, I'll have you know. Well, Ellie's family. But you take my point.

And Ellie, of course, freaked out. She went beserk.

"It's horrible," she cried. "**Horrible**. I can't believe that Tuffy could have done that. Thumper's been next door for years and years and years."

Sure. Thumper was a friend. I knew him well.

She turned on me.

28

Fiction

The Boy Who Cried Wolf
– a fable by Aesop retold by Susanna Davidson

The boy herded the flock up the hillside, swinging his bag on his back and whistling to himself. Day after day he watched over the sheep on the hill, sometimes daydreaming, sometimes singing, always longing for the hustle and bustle of the city, rather than the lonely hills of his home.

But today was going to be different. He had a brilliant trick in mind. No more boredom for him! He was going to make today exciting …

The boy waited until he reached the very top of the hill, standing on a rock above the grazing sheep. Then he opened his mouth and shouted as loudly as he could, "Wolf! Help! There's a wolf on the hill." And he pulled his horn from his bag and blew on it.

The villagers heard his cries. "A wolf?" they gulped. "Run! Run for the hills! We must save our sheep."

They came puffing and pounding up on the hill, old men and young boys, young girls and wives, waving sticks and brooms, rakes and rolling pins – anything they could find.

When they reached the top, they looked around. "Where's the wolf?" they cried.

The boy laughed and laughed. "There is no wolf," he replied. "I tricked you! Hee hee hee. I tricked you all. You looked so funny, panting up the hill …" He broke off to laugh some more.

The villagers were not happy.

"Don't do that again," the men scolded.

"Bad boy!" said the women, wagging their fingers at him.

And they stomped, one and all, back down the hill.

The boy waited until they were right at the very bottom. Then, with a sly smile, he climbed on his rock again and shouted. "Help! Wolf! There really **is** a wolf this time. Please come!" And he blew even louder and harder on his horn.

The villagers heard the urgency in his voice. "There must really be a wolf this time …" they said to each other.

Once again they turned and ran up the hill, puffing and panting till they reached the top.

The boy laughed and laughed until tears ran down his face. "I did it again!" he cried, jumping up and down. "I tricked you! I tricked you!"

"We'll not believe you a third time," said the villagers, before they took off for home. But the boy was too busy congratulating himself to listen.

He had just settled back against a tree, an apple in his hand, when he heard a stealthy pad, pad, padding noise on the soft earth, and the sound of twigs snapping underfoot. He looked up to see a large black wolf creeping out from behind a bush. He jumped up with a start.

"A wolf," he whispered to himself. "A real wolf."

With trembling hands, he reached for his horn and blew on it as hard as he could.

"Wolf! Wolf!" he cried, again and again. But no one came. His voice was soon hoarse from shouting, but no villagers appeared on the brow of the hill.

The boy could only watch in horror as the wolf devoured some sheep and scattered the rest across the hills.

As night fell, the boy slunk back down the hill, bringing no sheep behind him.

"Where's our flock? What have you done with our sheep?" demanded the villagers.

"A wolf came," sobbed the boy. "I called for you. Why didn't you come?"

"How could we know you were telling the truth?" the villagers replied. "You had tricked us twice before."

The boy hung his head in shame. "I'll never cry wolf again," he said.

Moral: No one believes a liar, even when he tells the truth.

Fiction

The Eagle and the Turtle – a fable by Aesop

The Turtle was not satisfied with his life. He wanted to stop being a turtle.

"I'm tired of swimming about in the sea and crawling about on the beach, getting nowhere in particular," he grumbled. "I want to be able to fly in the air like an eagle."

He spoke to the Eagle about it.

"You're not built for flying," the Eagle told the Turtle. "You haven't any wings."

"Don't worry about that," answered the Turtle. "I've watched how the birds do it. I've watched them soar and glide, skim and dive. Even if I haven't got wings, I can make my four flippers act like four stout oars in the air, the way I do in the water. Just get me up there, and you'll see I can fly as well as any of the birds – probably better! Besides, if you'll carry me as high as the clouds, I'll bring you lots of rare pearls from the sea."

The Eagle was tempted, and carried the Turtle up to a great height.

"Now, then!" cried the Eagle. "Fly!"

But the moment the Turtle was on his own, he fell from the sky. He fell like a stone, and on a stone he landed. He struck with such force that he smashed into little pieces.

Moral: Be satisfied with what you are.

Fiction

Snug   by Michael Morpurgo

Snug was Linda's cat. No one ever actually gave Linda the cat, they just grew up together. I don't really remember Linda being born, but apparently Snug turned up a few weeks earlier than she did. Dad found him wandering about, crying and mewing after a cat shoot in the barns – they shot them once in a while because they breed so fast. He found Snug crying round the calf pens. His mother must have been killed, or maybe she had run off.

Anyway, Dad picked him up and brought him home. He was so young that his eyes weren't open yet and Mum had to feed him warm milk with an eye dropper.

By the time Linda was born, Snug was a healthy kitten. Linda used to cry a lot – it's the first thing I remember about her – come to think of it, she still howls more than she should. Snug took to curling up underneath her cot when she was indoors, and by her pram if she was sleeping outside.

I first remember noticing that Linda and Snug went together when Linda was learning to walk. She was staggering about the kitchen doing a record-breaking run from the sink to the kitchen table, all five feet of it, when Snug sidled up to her and gently nudged her off balance into the dog bowl, which was full of water. We all fell about laughing while Linda sat there howling.

He adored Linda and followed her everywhere. He'd even go for walks with her, provided she left the dog at home. Linda used to bury her face in his fur and kiss him as if he was a doll, but he loved it and stretched himself out on his back waiting for his tummy to be tickled. Then he'd purr like a lion and shoot his claws in and out in blissful happiness.

Snug grew into a huge cat. I suppose you would call him a tabby cat, grey and dusty-white merging stripes with a tinge of ginger on his soft belly. He had great pointed ears, which he flicked and twitched even when he was asleep.

He came in every evening for his food, but he never really needed it, or if he did he certainly never showed it. He didn't often get into fights, and when he did, they hardly ever left a mark – he was either a coward or a champion.

He'd come in in the morning, after a night's hunting, full of mice and moles and voles, and lie down on Linda's bed, and purr himself to sleep, waking just in time for his evening meal, which Linda served him at five o'clock.

No one ever got angry with Snug and everyone who came to the house would admire him stalking through the long grass, or sunbathing by the vegetable patch, and Linda would preen herself whenever he was mentioned.

Linda could never understand why Snug killed birds. In the early summer he used to tease to death two or three baby thrushes or blackbirds a day. Linda very nearly went off him at this time every year. Only last summer he found a robin's nest at the bottom of a hedge – he'd been attracted by the cheeps. By the time we got there, he'd scooped out three baby robins and there were several speckled eggs lying broken and scattered. Linda didn't speak to him for a week, and I had to feed him. But they made it up, they always did.

Occasionally Snug wandered off into the barns and fields looking for a friendly she-cat. This must have taken a long time, because he disappeared sometimes for twenty-four hours or so – but never longer, except once.

Mum and Dad were home and Snug was late coming in. We'd had our bath and were sitting watching telly – **Tom and Jerry**, I think it was, because we always went to bed after that. There was a yowl outside the kitchen door, more like a dog in pain than a cat. Linda disappeared into the kitchen and I followed – I'd seen the **Tom and Jerry** before anyway. Linda opened the door and Snug came in, worming his way against the doorway. His head was hanging and his tail, which he usually held up straight, was drooping. One ear was covered in blood and there was a great scratch across his face. He'd been in a fight and he was badly hurt.

Linda picked him up gently and put him in his basket. "Get the TCP and some water ... quick!" she said.

Snug lay there panting while Linda cleaned up his wounds. I supplied the cotton wool and the TCP and when Linda had finished that, the Dettol.

She must have spent an hour or more nursing that cat, and all the time I didn't say a word to her: I knew she'd cry if I talked to her.

Mum came in after a bit to wash up. She bent over the basket. "He'll be all right, dear," she said. "It's not as bad as it looks. You'll see, he'll be right as rain by the morning. Why don't you see if he'll take some warm milk?"

Linda nodded. I knew she wouldn't do it herself; she'd have to turn round. She hated showing her face when she was upset. I put the milk on the stove and Mum cleared up. Linda put the saucer down by the basket and Snug went up to it almost immediately. He drank slowly, crouched over the milk, his pink tongue shooting clean into the saucer.

What happened next, happened so suddenly that none of us had time to react. Mum bent down to put some potato peel in the bin; she lifted it and opened the door to empty it. In a flash Snug was through the door, and we just stood there, the three of us, Mum clutching her bin, me holding the saucepan and Linda, her eyes red with crying.

Linda rushed after him, calling into the night. We all tried. Even Dad came away from the telly and called. But Snug would not come.

We tried to convince Linda that he'd be all right. Dad put his arm around her and stroked her hair before we went up to bed. "If he'd been really ill, love, he wouldn't have taken any milk." He was a great dad sometimes. "He'll be back tomorrow, you'll see."

We went off to school as usual the next morning. No one even mentioned Snug at breakfast. Usually we went along the road to school to meet up with Tom, but this morning Linda wanted to go through the fields. We left the house early and went off through the farm buildings where Snug used to hunt. Linda searched round the tractor sheds and calf pens, while I clambered over the straw in the Dutch barn. It was no good: there wasn't enough time. We had to get to school.

"It'll be all right, Lin," I said. "Don't worry." It was the best I could do.

School went slowly that day. Linda was even quieter than usual: she spent play-time looking over the fence into the orchard behind the playground, and during lessons she kept looking out of the window, and I could see her getting more and more worried.

Lunch came and went, and it started to rain: by the time we were let out it was pouring down. Linda grabbed her coat and rushed out. There was still no sign of Snug at home. We searched and called until it was dark and Mum came home from work. The time for his meal passed; still no Snug.

Dad came home a little later than usual. We were in the front room, Linda and I, and we heard him talking quietly to Mum in the kitchen.

We were mucking about trying to mend my train set on the floor when Dad came in. He didn't flop down in his armchair but stood there all tall and near the ceiling, and he hadn't taken his coat off. It was dripping on the carpet.

38

"Lin," he said. "I'm sorry, love, but we've found Snug. He's been killed, run over. Tom's father found him down by the main road. It must have been quick, he wouldn't have felt anything. I'm sorry, love."

Linda turned away.

"Are you sure it's him?" I said. "There's lots of cats like him about."

Linda ran out of the room and upstairs and Mum went up after her.

"It's him all right – I've got him in the shed outside. I thought we'd bury him tomorrow, if Lin wants us to." Dad sat down. "It's him all right, poor old thing."

"Can I have a look at him, Dad, just to be sure?" I said. I didn't feel like crying; somehow I couldn't feel sad enough. I was interested more than upset. It was strange because I really liked that cat.

Dad took me over to the shed and switched on the light. There he was, all stretched out in a huge cereal carton. He barely covered the bottom of it. His fur was matted and soaked. There was no blood or anything; he just lay there all still and his eyes closed.

"Well?" Dad mumbled behind me. "It's him, isn't it?" It **was** him, the same gingerish tummy, and the same tabby markings. He didn't look quite so big lying in that box.

"He's so still, Dad," I said. "Why isn't he all broken up after being run over? You'd think he'd be squashed or something."

"When you carry him, he doesn't feel right, but I expect he was thrown clear on impact," Dad said. "Go on now, you'd better go and see Lin."

When I got up to my bedroom, Mum was in with Linda and I could hear a lot of crying. I hate that: I never know what to say to people when they're like that. I went and lay on my bed and tried to feel sadder than I really was. I was more sorry about Lin than old Snug.

39

He'd had a fairly good run after all, lots of food and warmth and love. What more could a cat want? And for some reason I got to thinking of a party the mice would be holding in the Dutch barn that night to celebrate Snug's death.

I was down early in the morning before anyone else. I'd forgotten to feed the goldfish the night before. I was dropping the feed in the tank, when I heard Snug's voice outside the kitchen door. There was no mistake. It was his usual "purrrrrp... p... p" – a sort of demand for immediate entry. I wasn't hearing things either. I opened the door and in he came, snaking his way round the doorpost, as happy and contented with himself as ever.

I screamed upstairs, "He's here! He's back! Snug's back!"

Well of course they didn't take long to get down-stairs, and Linda was all weeping over him and examining him as if she couldn't believe it.

Dad came back from the shed in his slippers and dressing gown. "Lin, I'm sorry, love, but it's amazing: that cat's the spitting image of Snug. Honest he is."

Lin wasn't even listening, and I must admit I felt quite happy myself. It was a Saturday morning, Snug had come back from the dead and I was playing football that afternoon.

Dad and I buried the other cat after breakfast. We dug a hole in the woods on the other side of the stream and wrapped him in one of Dad's old gardening jackets.

When we got back, I saw Dawnie from school in the garden with Linda. Mum met us by the gate. "It was Dawn's cat," she said. "It's been missing for a couple of days and it's just like Snug. She wants to see where you've buried it."

Fiction

From **Cockadoodle-Doo, Mr Sultana!**
by Michael Morpurgo

Out in the countryside, the little red rooster was scratching around in the dusty farm track at the edge of the cornfield.

He scratched and he scratched. Suddenly there was something strange in the earth, something different, something very pretty that glistened and shone and twinkled in the sun. He tried eating it, but it didn't taste very good. So he dropped it. And then he had a sudden and brilliant idea.

"I know," he said to himself. "Poor old mistress mine loves pretty things. She's always saying so, and she's got nothing pretty of her own. I'll take it home for her. Then she won't be cross with me for running away, will she?"

But just as he picked it up again, along the farm track came the great fat Sultan on his horse, and in front of him, dozens of his servants, all of them crawling on their hands and knees in the dirt.

Closer and closer they came. All at once they spotted the little red rooster **and** the diamond button too, glinting in his beak.

"There my lord Sultan!" they cried. "LOOK! That little red rooster. He's got your diamond button."

42

"So that's what it is," the little red rooster said to himself.

The great fat Sultan rode up, scattering his servants hither and thither as he came. "Little Red Rooster," he said from high up on his horse. "I see you have my diamond button. I am your great and mighty Sultan. Give it to me at once. It's valuable, very valuable. And it's **mine**."

"I don't think so, Mr Sultana," replied the little red rooster, who had never in his life been frightened of anyone or anything. "COCKADOODLE-DOO, Mr Sultana. Finders keepers. If it's so valuable, then I'm going to give it to poor mistress mine. She needs it a lot more than you, I think. Sorry, Mr Sultana."

"**What**!" spluttered the Sultan. "Mr Sultana? How dare you speak to me like that? How dare you? Did you hear what that infernal bird called me? Fetch me that rooster. Fetch me my diamond button! Grab him! Grab that rooster!"

There was a frightful kerfuffle of dust and feathers … and SQUAWKING, as the Sultan's servants tried to grab the little red rooster. Whatever they did, they just could not catch him. In the end, the little red rooster ran off into the cornfield. But although he'd escaped their clutches, he was very cross with himself, for in all the kerfuffle he had dropped the diamond button.

Fiction

From **The Wind in the Willows (I)** by Kenneth Grahame

1. The River Bank

The Mole had been working very hard all the morning, spring-cleaning his little home.

First with brooms, then with dusters; then on ladders and steps and chairs, with a brush and pail of whitewash; till he had dust in his throat and eyes, and splashes of whitewash all over his black fur, and an aching back and weary arms. Spring was moving in the air above and in the earth below and around him, penetrating even his dark and lowly little house with its spirit of divine discontent and longing. It was small wonder, then, that he suddenly flung down his brush on the floor, said 'Bother!' and 'O blow!' and also 'Hang spring-cleaning!' and bolted out of the house without even waiting to put on his coat. Something up above was calling him imperiously, and he made for the steep little tunnel which answered in his case to the gravelled carriage-drive owned by animals whose residences are nearer to the sun and air. So he scraped and scratched and scrabbled and scrooged and then he scrooged again and scrabbled and scratched and scraped, working busily with his little paws and muttering to himself, 'Up we go! Up we go!' till at last, pop! His snout came out into the sunlight, and he found himself rolling in the warm grass of a great meadow.

'This is fine!' he said to himself. 'This is better than whitewashing!' The sunshine struck hot on his fur, soft breezes caressed his heated brow, and after the seclusion of the cellarage he had lived in so long the carol of happy birds fell on his dulled hearing almost like a shout. Jumping off all his four legs at once, in the joy of living and the delight of spring without its cleaning, he pursued his way across the meadow until he reached the hedge on the further side.

'Hold up!' said an elderly rabbit at the gap. 'Sixpence for the privilege of passing by the private road!' He was bowled over in an instant by the impatient and contemptuous Mole, who trotted along the side of the hedge chaffing the other rabbits as they peeped hurriedly from their holes to see what the row was about. 'Onion-sauce! Onion-sauce!' he remarked jeeringly, and was gone before they could think of a thoroughly satisfactory

reply. Then they all started grumbling at each other. 'How STUPID you are! Why didn't you tell him –' 'Well, why didn't YOU say –' 'You might have reminded him –' and so on, in the usual way; but, of course, it was then much too late, as is always the case.

It all seemed too good to be true. Hither and thither through the meadows he rambled busily, along the hedgerows, across the copses, finding everywhere birds building, flowers budding, leaves thrusting – everything happy, and progressive, and occupied. And instead of having an uneasy conscience pricking him and whispering 'whitewash!' he somehow could only feel how jolly it was to be the only idle dog among all these busy citizens. After all, the best part of a holiday is perhaps not so much to be resting yourself, as to see all the other fellows busy working.

He thought his happiness was complete when, as he meandered aimlessly along, suddenly he stood by the edge of a full-fed river. Never in his life had he seen a river before – this sleek, sinuous, full-bodied animal, chasing and chuckling, gripping things with a gurgle and leaving them with a laugh, to fling itself on fresh playmates that shook themselves free, and were caught and held again. All was a-shake and a-shiver – glints and gleams and sparkles, rustle and swirl, chatter and bubble. The Mole was bewitched, entranced, fascinated. By the side of the river he trotted as one trots, when very small, by the side of a man who holds one spell-bound by exciting stories; and when tired at last, he sat on the bank, while the river still chattered on to him, a babbling procession of the best stories in the world, sent from the heart of the earth to be told at last to the insatiable sea.

From **The Wind in the Willows (2)** by Kenneth Grahame

The Mole, who had been busily spring-cleaning his house, had come out for a rest.

As he sat on the grass and looked across the river, a dark hole in the bank opposite, just above the water's edge, caught his eye, and dreamily he fell to considering what a nice snug dwelling-place it would make for an animal with few wants and fond of a bijou riverside residence, above flood level and remote from noise and dust. As he gazed, something bright and small seemed to twinkle down in the heart of it, vanished, then twinkled once more like a tiny star. Something bright and small seemed to twinkle down in the heart of it, vanish, then twinkle once more like a tiny star. But it could hardly be a star in such an unlikely situation, and it was too glittering and too small for a glow-worm. Then, as he looked, it winked at him, and so declared itself to be an eye; and a small face began gradually to grow up round it, like a frame round a picture.

A brown little face, with whiskers.

A grave round face, with the same twinkle in its eye that had first attracted his notice.

Small neat ears and thick silky hair.

It was the Water Rat!

…

The Rat said nothing, but stooped and unfastened a rope and hauled on it, then lightly stepped into a little boat which the Mole had not observed. It was painted blue outside and white within, and was just the size for two animals; and the Mole's whole heart went out to it at once, even though he did not yet fully understand its uses.

The Rat sculled smartly across and made fast. Then he held up his forepaw as the Mole stepped gingerly down. 'Lean on that!' he said: 'Now then, step lively!' and the Mole to his surprise and rapture found himself actually seated in the stern of a real boat.

'This has been a wonderful day!' he said, as the Rat shoved off and took to the sculls again. 'Do you know, I've never been in a boat before in all my life.'

Fiction

From Stowaway! (1) by Julia Jarman

This historical adventure tells the story of a young Tudor boy in the sixteenth century, and his dream to sail with the famous Captain Francis Drake.

1. Decision time!

It was a cold November afternoon and a wind had got up. Dickon looked longingly at the ships in Plymouth harbour, five of them, white sails billowing. There was the **Marigold**, the **Benedict**, the **Swan**, the **Elizabeth** and the flagship, the **Pelican**.

How Dickon envied his best friend, Tib, who was aboard the **Pelican**, for the famous Francis Drake was its captain – Francis Drake, England's greatest sailor and friend of Good Queen Bess. Francis Drake who had come back from the Spanish Main, his ship laden with gold. And now he was setting out on another exciting voyage – with Tib as his cabin boy.

Dickon gritted his teeth to stop the tears. He'd tried to get a job, but the second mate had taken one look at his lame leg and said, "Sorry, lad. We only take the fit and able. You couldn't climb the mainmast."

"I could …" But the second mate hadn't listened. Instead, he said to Tib, "You'll do. You look like a strong lad." So Tib would have gold for his mother when the ship returned to Plymouth. Dickon would have nothing, and his poor widowed mother had eight boys to feed.

Dickon was suddenly jolted out of his misery by a loud voice.

"Here, boy, carry this!" A young gentleman in a leather doublet had dropped a bag at Dickon's feet.

Then a gentleman with dark hair and beard called out from the **Pelican**.

"Cousin John! Not a moment too soon. We sail at five!" Dickon couldn't believe his eyes. It was Francis Drake! It must be. He wore a gold chain around his neck.

"Cousin Francis!" The young gentleman ran up the gangway.

Dickon ran after him, carrying the bag. He **could** run and he could climb. He could do lots of things.

Francis Drake and his cousin, John, hugged each other. "Put your mattress and bag in the grand cabin, then join me," said the Captain. John Drake turned to Dickon. "Come on, lad!" Dickon followed him down the ladder eagerly, for he'd made an important decision.

Where to hide? That was the question. The hold would be best. Luckily everyone was busy loading the ship or tightening the rigging, so no one took much notice of him. Leaving John Drake in the grand cabin, Dickon headed back to the ladder as the ship started to rock. The tide was on the turn. Soon the ship would leave. He must be quick. Down the ladder he went – and down again – and again. The lower he got, the darker it got. Now he could hear men heaving cargo into place, but only see their shapes. Dodging behind the ladder, he heard someone above shout orders.

"Cast off the lines!"

He felt the ship float free. They were off! Now men scrambled over him, up the ladder. "Let's get on deck, lads! Let's see the last of old England!"

The last of old England! As Dickon wedged himself between a barrel and a bale of linen, he felt a thrill of excitement.

2. Discovered!

But later that night Dickon was scared. A storm had got up and the ship was rolling from side to side. He could hear the wind howling and feel the sea crashing against the sides. Dickon was hungry too. Where would he get food? What would happen if he were found? What if the ship sank? How would his mother know where he was? Then the ship nearly keeled over, throwing him out of his hiding place. Dickon saw a man with a swaying lantern peering down at him.

"What are you doing here, boy?"

"Hiding, sir." He was too hungry to lie.

"Captain, not sir. Don't you know the punishment for entering the hold?"

Dickon recognised the man. It was Captain Drake. He shouted at Dickon, "If you've been stealing, boy, you will have your hand nailed to the mast."

"I haven't been stealing. I wanted a job."

"And do you still?" said the captain, more gently, now.

"Yes, Captain, I want gold for my mother, so she can feed my brothers."

Now the famous man stooped to peer closely at Dickon. "Aren't you sea-sick, boy?"

"No, Captain. I'm too hungry to be sick."

Drake laughed and pulled Dickon to his feet. "There are forty men above, all as sick as pigs, except you and me. So, lad, if we survive this storm, you have a job. I just hope you like adventure."

They did all survive, though the storm raged for three days. Dickon became a cabin boy to Francis Drake, along with his friend Tib.

"It's the best job on board," laughed Tib, "looking after the captain!"

From **Stowaway!** (2) by Julia Jarman

3. Mutiny ... almost!

Not everyone on the **Pelican** was happy about going to the Indies. Some of the crew grumbled when Drake ordered them to sail south-west. Their grumbles grew when for weeks there was no sight of land. Then the little fleet seemed stuck, for there was no wind, none at all. And it was hot – scorching hot – the sun was like fire. It was because they were near the line, some old hands said, the line around the middle of the world. When Dickon and Tib could bear to go on deck they couldn't see any line, just sea, huge fish and enormous birds. Sailors were dying from the heat and Preacher Fletcher was kept busy with funeral services.

As Dickon saw bodies being thrown into the sea he began to wonder if he would ever get home, and his dreams of riches began to fade.

But soon afterwards a fair wind got up and spirits rose on the **Pelican**.

"Gold **will** be ours!" Drake said in a ringing speech to the crew. "For we are on course again! We have only to get through the Magellan Straits, then we'll be in sight of Spanish galleons!"

Only get through the Magellan Straits! Dickon had heard about them. Criss-crossed by dangerous currents, they were like tunnels with mountains on either side.

Soon after his speech, Drake ordered them to dock on the east coast of Brasilia. He wanted to get repairs done before the dreaded straits. He also decided to repaint the **Pelican** in red and yellow, the colours of his backer, Sir Christopher Hatton. He renamed the ship too. From now on she was the **Golden Hinde**. The carpenter had to carve a new ship's head in the shape of a hind. Drake said they would coat it with Spanish gold as soon as they had boarded a Spanish galleon and taken all of its treasure!

As he and Tib helped paint the handrail on the upper deck, Dickon started to get a little scared again. Wasn't it unlucky to change the name of a ship? Preacher Fletcher had blessed it, but they'd still got to get through the Magellan Straits.

4. A challenge

Dickon needn't have worried. With Drake at the helm the **Golden Hinde** sailed through safely in sixteen days. The **Marigold** and the **Elizabeth** were not far behind.

"Thanks be to God!" cried Drake as they entered the South Sea. "We are the first Englishmen to come this way! And now the fun begins. The first man or boy to spy a Spanish treasure ship will get a link of this!"

He swung his gold chain above his head. There was a race for the rigging. Tib ran to the mainmast and started climbing.

Dickon ran to the foremast, shouting, "Race you to the top, Tib!"

A boy called Will ran to the mizzenmast. They all began climbing, and the crew began to clap rhythmically.

Dickon had been practising. He climbed as fast as he could, but when he was only half way Tib yelled, "First!" The crew cheered. They cheered again when Will reached the top of the mizzen. And they cheered Dickon when he reached the top of the foremast, but he couldn't help feeling disappointed. With his lame leg, would he ever be fast enough to win a link of Drake's golden chain? He scanned the horizon. There was nothing wrong with his eyes. Perhaps he would be the first to see a Spanish galleon? But all he saw was the coast stretching north as far as he could see. No ships at all.

Then Tib yelled, "Storm clouds in the south! Moving towards us! Fast!"

It was a huge bank of black cloud, moving ever so fast. They scrambled down to tell the others. An older hand agreed with them. A huge storm was on its way.

Captain Drake shouted orders.

"Batten down the hatches! Shorten the sails! Then lash yourselves to the ship!"

"Above or below?" Tib said to Dickon.

"Above," said Dickon. "I want to see it."

But when the storm came he couldn't see anything. He could only feel the icy waves crashing over him. As darkness fell he felt the ship flying through the water, and all he could do was pray.

Fiction

From **Sophie's Rules** by Keith West

SCENE 1

(Dana's new to Deepvale School. She notices Sophie, Anna and Jade. They're sitting in the classroom, having arrived early. She walks nervously up to them.)

DANA: (shyly) Hi.

SOPHIE: (turning round to look at Dana) Hi. What are you doing in our classroom? You new here?

DANA: Yes, I'm Dana. I've just arrived here – we've just moved in. What's your name?

SOPHIE: My name's Sophie and my mates are Anna (pointing to the other girl) and Jade.

ANNA: You can sit with us if you like.

(Sophie scowls.)

DANA: (enthusiastically) Thanks!

SOPHIE: I can tell you're not from around here. You're different.

DANA: Mum and I have just moved into Wordsworth Crescent.

SOPHIE: (smirking) Wordsworth Crescent?

JADE: Isn't that where Natalie Shanks lives?

SOPHIE: (nastily) Longshanks, sheepshanks. (to Dana) She's weird. We don't like people from Wordsworth Crescent, (to Jade and Anna) do we?

(Dana looks nervous and swallows hard.)

JADE: No.

ANNA: We don't.

SOPHIE: (pointing at Dana's clothes) Why aren't you in school uniform, like us? I wouldn't be seen dead in what you're wearing.

(Dana looks down at her clothes.)

JADE: (nastily) Yeah, what's so special about you? Why do you have to be different?

DANA: Because –

JADE: Because you're from Wordsworth Crescent, that's why. They're all nerds down that part of town.

DANA: (upset) No … I …

(Sophie and Jade laugh. Anna looks at Dana with a hint of sympathy.)

SOPHIE: What did you and your mates do at your old school? Play sports or anything? We play sports down at the big field on Saturdays.

DANA: We used to do drama. There was a drama club at …

JADE: (bored) We don't play games.

DANA: Drama isn't just playing games …

SOPHIE: Could have fooled us, eh, Jade? (to Jade, indicating Dana) Just like Natalie!

JADE: (smirking) What?

SOPHIE: She's like Natalie … you know … funny.

DANA: (worried) Don't you do drama? It's really good fun.

(The three girls shake their heads.)

DANA: I don't have to do drama. It's just … that's what we did at our old school.

SOPHIE: (mocking) A school for funny people.

ANNA: We talk about clothes, fashion, pop stars, music … that kind of stuff.

DANA: (trying to smile) That's cool. I like talking too. I like fashion.

JADE: (pointing at Dana's clothes) Looks like it!

(Jade and Sophie laugh.)

SOPHIE: (to Anna and Jade) Come on, let's go next door. We'll see Brad and his mates. (glaring at Dana) They must be funny where she comes from. She speaks in a silly way.

DANA: But –

SOPHIE: (to Anna) They must breed people like Natalie where she comes from.

(The three girls walk out of the room, leaving Dana alone. She looks down at the table and puts her head in her hands.)

Fiction

From **In the Rue Bel Tesoro** by Lin Coghlan

This is the beginning of a play about children living in a country where soldiers are fighting and ordinary people are struggling to survive.

SCENE 1

(A busy train station crowded with travellers. Sasha and Omar arrive pushing an old-fashioned pram and carrying a bag stuffed with belongings.)

SASHA: Don't say anything, Omar; let me do the talking.

OMAR: (into the pram) You've got to keep quiet, Valentine, we're in the station now.

(They approach a soldier checking documents at the entrance to the platform.)

SOLDIER: Papers?

SASHA: (handing over the papers) We're going to meet our mother. She's waiting for us.

SOLDIER: The baby – his pass?

SASHA: He's … a new baby, he doesn't have one.

SOLDIERS: No papers, I can't let you through.

(Fran arrives with a huge suitcase and pushes in.)

FRAN: Please – let an old woman by! My bad hip! My feet!

SOLDIER: (unmoved) Papers?

(Fran gives him her papers as the children watch.)

SOLDIER: Go through.

(Fran hurries through the barrier. Sasha grabs Omar and drags him after Fran, getting away from the soldier.)

SOLDIER: Hey, you! Come back!

(Sasha and Omar disappear into the crowd.)

SCENE 2

(Fran staggers into the train compartment with her bundles.)

SASHA: Please, madam, if we could stay with you, we're on our own …

FRAN: Oh no – impossible. I must have my space.

SASHA: The soldiers don't stop old people so much when they have children.

FRAN: I don't like babies.

OMAR: It isn't a baby – it's a dog.

(Sasha looks at him furiously.)

From **Ade Adepitan: A Paralympian's Story**
by Ade Adepitan

The trek of my life

In 2005, I was asked to trek with a group of disabled people across Central America. Twelve of us, all with different disabilities, were going to trek from one side of Nicaragua to the other side. We had to get our own water, make our own meals, set up our own camp and stuff like that. We had a guide who was a former SAS guy and one local guy. It was probably the most amazing thing I've ever done in my life. It was unbelievable – it took us a month and I lost six kilograms in weight. There were two of us in wheelchairs and although we had specially-designed chairs with chunkier tyres to help us, they still kept falling apart. By the end of the trek, we'd had so many punctures that we ended up putting vine leaves in the tyres instead of air.

We'd trek every day for seven or eight hours, with the aim of travelling 10 to 12 kilometres in a day. We were primarily in thick rainforest, so we couldn't see more than three to four metres ahead and it was just nothing but trees, mud, broken leaves and these crazy howler monkeys cracking nuts from the trees. Then about an hour before it got dark, we'd have to find somewhere close to a river to set up camp. Then we'd get up at six o'clock the next morning and carry on trekking.

Non-Fiction

The Day the Helicopters Came by Rachel Anderson

This story is about how frightening it was for a child when an army invaded a village during the Vietnam War in the 1960s.

We had a cow for milk, some hens, and a goat. We harvested enough rice and vegetables for our family and the rest my mother sent downriver to market in the city.

Then one day the helicopters came. We watched them circle, then bump down, one after another in rapid succession, onto our vegetable gardens. The men jumped out and ran, bent double as though themselves afraid of being fired on, over melons, beans, celery, trampling with their boots on whatever produce hadn't already been destroyed by shells. "We must go in," said my mother, and she hurried us inside. But my grandmother was in a trance, dazed by three nights in the shelter. My mother sat her down gently on the stool and gave her the baby to hold while she saw to the clearing up.

The room was suddenly darkened by a huge mass, higher than the door lintel, blocking out the light. He was so tall that he had to stoop to stand in the doorway, and even then the top of his helmet was lost in the grass thatch.

"Where's your husband, lady?" he shouted. My mother snatched the baby back from my grandmother and held it to her tightly. The man instinctively twitched his gun back at her. He was very frightened.

"Your husband! Where is he?"

He didn't see me. I was in the folds of my father's jacket hanging on a peg. But as I flattened myself more against the wall I knocked an earthenware dish down from the shelf. It clattered to the floor.

64

Snake in the Grass

The snake cannot be trusted,
Sliding through sand and sea,
Sneaking through the bushes,
Or slithering round a tree.

For when you least expect it,
He'll raise his head and strike,
His fangs dripping with venom,
Pierces like a spike.

He'll often kill at random,
Not just the things he'll eat,
Like fish and snails and worms
And mostly anything with feet.

Some snakes will hug you, not in love,
But to squeeze you free of life,
Some will even eat their family,
Mother, sister, wife.

You'll often find this serpent,
Curled up beneath a stone,
Wondering why he has no friends,
And is always on his own.

Valerie Bloom

Poetry
Kob Antelope

A creature to pet and
spoil like a child.
Smooth-skinned
Stepping cautiously
in the lemon grass …
The eyes
like a bird's.
The head
beautiful like carved wood …
Your neck seems long,
so very long
to the greedy hunter.

**Anon. (Yoroba),
an unknown Nigerian poet**

From **Angry Arthur** by Hiawyn Oram

"No," said his mother, "it's too late. Go to bed."

"I'll get angry," said Arthur.

"Get angry," said his mother.

So he did. Very, very angry.

He got so angry that his anger became a stormcloud exploding thunder and lightning and hailstones.

"That's enough," said his mother. But it wasn't.

Arthur's anger became a hurricane hurling rooftops and chimneys and church spires.

"That's enough," said his father. But it wasn't.

Arthur's anger became a typhoon tipping whole towns into the sea.

"That's enough," said his grandfather. But it wasn't.

Arthur's anger became a universequake and the earth and the moon and the stars and the planets, Arthur's country and Arthur's town, his street, his house, his garden and his bedroom were nothing more than bits in space.

Arthur sat on a bit of Mars and thought. He thought and thought. "Why was I so angry?" he thought. He never did remember. Can you?

My Hair as Black as Dirty Coal

My hair as black as dirty coal,
My eyes sizzle like fried eggs in a pan,
My nose breathes heavily like a charging wild bull.
Because:
(My brother …)

My mouth breathing fire like a dragon.
My stomach going in and out,
I clench my fists hard like compressing a lemon
Until all the juice comes out.

(kicked my …)

My anger bubbling inside,
Ready to fire out of my head.
I think I'm Arnold
 Schwarzenegger.
My feet heat up ready to kick out
And then I burst out.

(ball over the fence!!)

Bertie Thomson

Non-fiction

From **Breath** by Claire Llewellyn

Work those lungs!

When you're running fast, your muscles are working hard. They need more oxygen to keep going and so you puff and breathe more deeply. You breathe through your mouth as well as your nose to take in extra air. At the same time, your heart beats faster. It's delivering oxygen-rich blood to your muscles as quickly as it can.

Puffing and panting is good for you! Exercise helps your lungs grow stronger so they supply more oxygen to the body. It's important to be active every day. Running, dancing, skipping and swimming are much better for you than sitting still, and will strengthen your lungs.

Did you know?
Playing some musical instruments, such as the mouth organ, trumpet or recorder, helps to make your lungs stronger.

The brain and breathing

When you swim and dive underwater, you have to hold your breath. It's impossible to do this for long: your brain drives you up to the surface to fill your lungs with air.

Your brain is always in control of your breathing. It knows how much oxygen you have in your blood. If you're active and using a lot of oxygen, your brain orders your chest muscles to work harder and breathe in more. If you're asleep and using very little oxygen, your brain orders your muscles to work more slowly.

Your brain itself needs oxygen to work. If your brain runs out of oxygen, it stops working properly. This is very dangerous: after just five minutes without oxygen, brain cells begin to die.

An adult's breathing rate	
Action	**Breaths per minute**
Sleeping	12–15
Normal breathing	12–20
After exercise	40

Did you know?
An adult's lungs hold about five litres of air. A tall person's lungs hold more than a shorter person's. A man's lungs hold more than a woman's.

Non-fiction
Feathered Record Breakers

Biggest alive
The giant of the bird world is the ostrich, from Africa. It grows up to 2.7 metres and can weigh over 155 kilograms. Its eggs are also the biggest, weighing in at 1.5 kilograms.

Heaviest extinct bird
The roc, or elephant bird, lived in Madagascar until 300 years ago. It weighed over 420 kilograms, and laid eggs 7 times as big as the ostrich.

Heaviest flier
The African Kori bustard has been known to weigh 18 kilograms.

Tallest extinct bird
Some species of the New Zealand Moa grew to over 4 metres, but they died out about 700 years ago.

Fastest flier
Spine-tailed swifts can reach 170 kilometres per hour.

Fastest runner
Ostriches can run at 65 kilometres per hour.

Greatest wingspan
The wandering albatross has a wingspan up to 3 metres.

Smallest bird
The bee hummingbird measures less than 6 centimetres from beak to tail and weighs 2 grams.

Deepest divers
Emperor penguins have been known to reach depths of over 250 metres.

74

Non-fiction

What is the Sun?

The Sun is a star. It is the nearest star to Earth, which is why it seems much bigger than any other star, but really the Sun is quite a small star. Some stars, that are much further away, are thousands of times bigger than the Sun.

The Sun is a huge ball of fiery gas. It is 150 million kilometres from Earth, and without it there would be no light or warmth on Earth. If the Sun did not give us light and heat there would be no life on Earth, so the Sun is very important to us. We are not its only planet, though; it has eight others.

It takes about 365 days, or one year, to travel once around the Sun.

Poetry

What is ... The Sun?

The Sun is an orange dinghy
sailing across a calm sea.

It is a gold coin
dropped down a drain in heaven.

It is a yellow beach ball
kicked high into the summer sky.

It is a red thumb-print
on a sheet of pale blue paper.

It is the gold top from a milk bottle
floating on a puddle.

Wes Magee

From **Black Holes** by Anna Claybourne

What do black holes do?

When an object gets close to a black hole, it's pulled faster and faster into the middle of it. This happens because black holes have very strong gravity.

Gravity is a pulling force. All objects have it and the bigger the object, the stronger its gravity. On Earth, gravity is what makes an orange fall when you throw it. It makes rivers flow downhill and skateboards zoom down a ramp. Gravity holds each person in place on the ground. Without gravity, we'd float off into space.

When you're on a slope, the pulling force of gravity drags you towards the bottom. If you're on wheels, or the surface is slippery, you zoom downhill.

When the gravity in a black hole pulls on objects, it doesn't just move them towards the middle of the black hole. It's so strong, and pulls so hard, it changes their shape.

The gravity in a black hole stretches and squishes objects as they get sucked in, making them longer and thinner. In the middle of the black hole, gravity compresses them so tightly, they get crushed down to nothing. If you looked inside a black hole you wouldn't see suns and moons floating about inside it – they have been crushed so small, you wouldn't see anything at all.

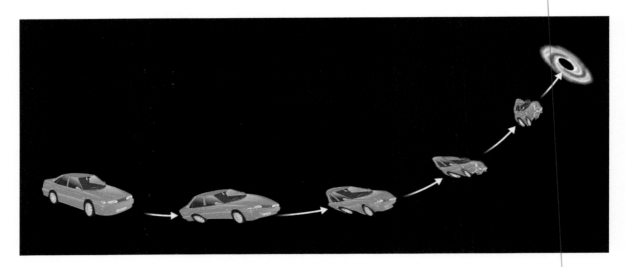

Black holes are small but dense

All the stuff that gets sucked into a black hole is compressed into a tiny dot in the middle. That dot is smaller than a grape. It's smaller than a grain of sand. In fact, it's so small it takes up no space at all!